B. P. Pratten

Speeches and Letters in Support of the Candidacy of Joseph

H. Choate for United States Senator

B. P. Pratten

Speeches and Letters in Support of the Candidacy of Joseph H. Choate for United States Senator

ISBN/EAN: 9783337154141

Printed in Europe, USA, Canada, Australia, Japan

Cover: Foto ©ninafisch / pixelio.de

More available books at **www.hansebooks.com**

AND LETTERS

SUPPORT OF THE CANDIDACY
OF

JOSEPH H. CHOATE

FOR

UNITED STATES SENATOR,

BEING PART OF THE PROCEEDINGS

AT THE

MASS MEETING OF REPUBLICAN VOTERS

D IN CARNEGIE MUSIC HALL, NEW YORK CITY, ON THE

EVENING OF WEDNESDAY, DECEMBER 23, 1896,

UNDER THE AUSPICES OF THE

CONTENTS.

ADDRESS OF EDMUND WETMORE, Esq.

Fellow Citizens:

This meeting has been called to endorse as a candidate for the office of United States Senator, that life-long Republican, that eloquent advocate, that patriotic citizen and gifted man, Joseph H. Choate.

We propose his name, because we believe him pre-eminently fitted, in ability and character, to uphold the principles of the Republican Party and worthily represent the State of New York in our national councils.

It is a time when that party has a peculiar need for the services of its ablest and strongest men. After a momentous political crisis, it has once more been entrusted with the controlling power in the government of the nation. It receives that power not only from the hands of its customary supporters, but from those who, having been its longest and most earnest opponents, nevertheless when the safety of the country was at stake, put aside every consideration of party name or party antipathies, and worked and voted for the Republican candidates.

Coming into power under these circumstances, it is under a double responsibility to fulfill its pledges, and deal with the vast interests committed to its charge, with the wisdom and fidelity the country has a right to expect. And it can do that only by a steadfast adherence to its own principles. Our Democratic allies who so patriotically aided our triumph would despise us if we did otherwise. These principles will form the guide by which its representatives in Congress and the Senate will endeavor to mould the legislation that is to affect the country.

To aid effectively in that work requires sound judgment, ability in debate, power to rightly comprehend the grave and difficult questions upon the wise solution of which the very safety of the republic may depend, and an integrity of purpose that inspires public confidence and secures the influence that public confidence can alone bestow. We have the rare satisfaction of finding in Mr. Choate one who fulfills all these requirements, and therefore we advocate his election.

That distinguished Democrat, Mr. Hewitt, in an interview two days since, lamented the decline of statesmanship in the United States Senate; we want to do what lies in our power to supply the deficiency so far as concerns the representatives of the great State of New York.

I will not usurp the time of the eloquent speakers who are to follow me in expanding the theme of Mr. Choate's fitness for the office for which we propose him, but I do wish to add a word as to the healthful sign of improvement in our political life that is evidenced by the awakened interest that our citizens take in every effort to secure better government. Men may differ widely as to the wisdom, and are often prone to doubt the sincerity of those who are active in that work and disagree as to the expediency or effectiveness of what they propose, but no man can deny that the final preservation of popular government requires that the great body of the citizens, each according to his convictions, abilities and opportunities, should take an active part in the performance of political duties. And my profound conviction is that the place where political duties most urgently call for performance is within party lines. Government by party is not perfect, but it is the only method of government which, up to this time, has been developed, or is possible in our republic, and it is the one with which we have to deal and under which our national progress has been made and our national institutions preserved. And that party is strongest that, in the men it selects for its offices and the measures it carries through, reflects most truly the genuine public opinion that prevails among its members.

If this truth had been perceived by our political opponents; if the Democratic party had had leaders instead of managers, it would not have fallen into the bog of repudiation at Chicago and left those who represented its honesty and intelligence and patriotism no choice but to leave its ranks.

When, therefore, a Republican Legislature is about to enter upon the important and solemn duty of choosing a Senator of the United States, I know no method more appropriate, no means more effective for indicating candidates whose choice would be welcome to the party and useful to the State, than the testimony of their fellow-townsmen in public meeting assembled to the esteem and confidence in which they are held. That is what we have assembled for to-night as regards our fellow-townsman, Mr. Choate. And the esteem and confidence that we feel and express extend throughout the State. Mr. Choate stands for no faction. The character and the number of the Republicans of this State who desire his election are such and so great that, even if their opinion were overruled, it could not be despised. His candidacy will receive the consideration and carry the weight that his eminence and character deserve, and no one can be presented for the suffrages of the Legislature more worthy of the high office for which he is proposed. It is an advance towards better politics when men, such as he, become candidates. To support him is a badge of good citizenship; to elect him will be an honor to the State.

ADDRESS OF WILLIAM D. GUTHRIE, Esq.

Fellow Republicans:

Your presence here from all quarters of the city on such a stormy night proclaims that the objects which we advocate have made a deep impression on your hearts and that the people have at last been aroused to a sense of impending danger.

The men who have summoned this mass meeting of republican voters expect me, I assume, to state in detail the issues we are debating, and to invite an expression of public opinion. They surely conceive it to be impossible that any republican majority, mindful of the traditions of our great party, can be deaf to the voice and the wishes of their constituents. They cannot believe that the members of our legislature will disregard the admonitions of duty, conscience and patriotism, or defiantly reject the instructions of the voters who elected them. Therefore, it is the purpose of this meeting to enlighten the representatives and agents of the people at Albany as to public opinion and to instruct them as to our choice.

We are assembled to discuss in the open a great question of vital public interest ; to emphasize an issue of political liberty which is of immeasurable importance to the whole nation ; to secure the election of a worthy representative of this State in the national senate ; to save the republican party from taking a step which would inevitably lead to its defeat and ruin, and to redeem the State of New York, so far as we can, from the odium and disgrace of further boss rule.

Intimidated by no threats, dispirited by no calculated chances of success, seeking and expecting no aid or inspiration except that which is born of the conviction that we are in the right, we come here without malice and without factional purpose to submit our views of political rights and duties for the consideration of our fellow republicans.

There never has been a time in the history of this nation when the federal senate stood in greater need of the highest order of ability, character and patriotism, when it was more necessary to have able and upright representation for local as well as for national interests, for the present as well as for the future, for ourselves as for posterity.

The great State of New York, with its immense population, its vast wealth, its incalculable commercial interests, its seven millions of people, has no larger representation and no greater voice in the senate at Washington than the smallest State of only fifty thousand inhabitants. New York has more than one hundred times the population of Nevada, yet each State has two senators. The uneven development of the country has rendered such a distribution of political power grossly, absurdly unfair, but that feature of the Constitution cannot be changed by amendment without the consent of the States. It is, however, always within the power of the people of the more populous States to counterbalance, in some measure at least, this great disadvantage by sending as their representatives to the national senate the foremost and best equipped of their statesmen.

We have among us, ever ready to perform any duty that patriotism dictates, an ideal candidate—one of the greatest of our public men, a most conspicuous and a unique figure in the eyes of the country, the leader of the American bar, the successor of Webster as the foremost constitutional lawyer of the day, an orator of the highest rank, a scholar and statesman of the broadest culture, a sturdy American of that sturdy New England type, a staunch republican—a man of splendid

talents and unblemished honor, to whom jealousy or
hatred can deny no title to glory. If the people wish
to send such a delegate to the national senate, they can
do so in the person of the Honorable Joseph H. Choate,
the true friend, the chivalrous advocate, the lion-hearted
patriot, a man whom no fear can deter and no miserable
calculations of expediency or failure hinder from the
performance of duty. When asked to make this fight
against bossism, he was begged by many friends not to
enter the lists, because it seemed a forlorn hope. The
substance of his answer was as Samuel Adams would
have answered, if I may apply Webster's ringing words,
" My judgment approves this movement, my whole
heart is in it, my patriotic feelings impel me ; all that
I have and all that I am and all that I hope in this
life I am ready here to stake upon it. If I were so
cowardly as to falter now when asked to stand up and
make this fight, simply because I am not guaranteed
success or freedom from inevitable political abuse, may
my tongue cleave to the roof of my mouth!" A distinguished lawyer advised him to decline to be a candidate, because the result was doubtful, and failure
would dim his prestige and his reputation. I can
well imagine Choate turning on him, his face glow-
ing with indignation, and saying : " If I knew now
that not one man in the republican caucus would
dare to vote for me, I should run and continue to
run, because I believe it to be my duty to protest
against the present political conditions in this State
—a condition that shocks every national instinct
in me and makes my blood boil with indignant revolt." You all know Choate, whose words have thus
thrilled you. You have seen that grand and stately
figure, a born leader of men, " for dignity composed and
high exploit." If Joseph H. Choate, after his great
career at the bar, and in spite of the affliction that has

so lately darkened his home, is ready to step forward and lead us, shall we pause and hesitate to follow?

From every corner of the State, from every fireside of those plain people who make up the strength and stability of the republican party, from every State in the Union, the mere suggestion of the possibility of Mr. Choate's candidacy has brought forth expressions of patriotic hope and longing. Everywhere he is proclaimed to be an ideal candidate and the people's choice. On all sides, even by his enemies, his brilliant talents are conceded, his peculiar and great capacity for the office undisputed, his high character admired, the vital necessity for just such a statesman admitted. Why can we not have him as our senator? Because, as we are told, even if the republican voters clamored for his election, it is now too late; because the legislature is said to be owned by a man who has not yet dared to come out publicly as an avowed candidate; because they say the legislature of the State of New York is pledged—enslaved—and cannot break its chains. I deny it. It must be false. It is false. The republican legislature shall refute that slander by voting for the candidate of the people.

It is objected that the party cannot send Mr. Choate to the United States Senate because he is not in favor of protection; but they all know he has been an out-and-out protectionist for forty years, and has always been with his party on that question, on the currency, on every fundamental principle. I shall read you a resolution offered by Mr. Choate at a meeting of the Union League Club in December, 1888, shortly after Harrison's election, and leave you to judge whether Choate is a protectionist:

> "*Resolved*, that the decisive verdict of the American people in favor of maintaining the system of protection of our domestic industries, under which we have enjoyed such uniform and marvellous prosperity, has perpetuated that

system as our cardinal national policy. That returning to power on this issue on which the canvass has been fought and won, the republicans are bound to adapt the legislation of Congress to carry out the declared wishes of the people, and to fulfill their pledges given in successive national conventions, to reduce taxation to the measure of the public needs, and to reform and revise the existing tariff, to prune away its extravagances, and to readjust its burdens, with a careful regard to the preservation and protection of our manufactures, which have been fostered and maintained by its aid."

The next objection is that Mr. Choate criticised the McKinley Bill. He did. When that measure was being discussed, Mr. Choate insisted that some of its items were too high ; that the increases in many instances were too great and ought at least to have been gradual; that in any event the act should not go into effect for at least six months, and that any tariff act that made radical alterations should take effect only after a reasonable period, so that the trades affected might be able to prepare and adjust their business accordingly. Such was the view at the time of other leading republicans, including Mr. Blaine. Mr. Choate then urged that too sudden and radical a change would surely lead to defeat at the approaching congressional elections, and that such a policy might cost us the control of the government in 1892. In a word, he agreed with Mr. Blaine. You all recall the disaster of 1890 and the loss of the presidency in 1892. What think you of the statesmanship of the man who had the wisdom, the foresight and the courage to say to his party that they were making a mistake ? It was an example of the farsighted broad views of public affairs which we need in the senate to-day. He was sound then, as we know he is sound to-day. And there is one man in the United States who above all others will acknowledge that if the advice of Choate and Blaine had been followed in 1890, the great defeat of that year and of 1892, and the subsequent birth of Bryanism might have been averted.

We learn by experience, and the lesson in this instance was an awful one to the country. Can any man doubt that Mr. McKinley would say that Mr. Choate was then right?

Another objection urged is that Mr. Choate has held aloof from practical politics, and is not, therefore, a good judge of men and things. As a trafficker in office, a distributer of spoils, a solicitor of patronage at the public crib, he is lacking and will be found wanting. But in true statesmanship, in familiarity with our history, in power to perceive the currents of national feeling, in ability to devise wise, effective and beneficial legislation, no man living surpasses him. Those who have heard his great forensic arguments before the Supreme Court at Washington, in cases of constitutional law, know him to be one of the best informed public men of the day. His discernment of popular tendencies is equal to Blaine's power. It was he who, weeks before any one in the East championed the cause, stepped forward in McKinley's support. Long in advance of the development of McKinley's strength, Mr. Choate came out for him, boldly declaring that the people demanded and insisted upon the nomination of McKinley. Here is an article printed in the *Sun* of March 20th (previously published in the *Commercial Advertiser*), three months before the St. Louis Convention met :

"I think McKinley is the coming man," said Mr. Choate. "His selection seems almost a foregone conclusion. Why, his boom is sweeping across the country with irresistible force. He stands for Americanism, pure and simple."·

"What do you mean by Americanism?"

"Protection and the independence of America. The wave of patriotic feeling growing out of the Venezuelan and Cuban controversies which has swept across the country will naturally cluster around McKinley's boom. McKinley stands first and foremost for protection to the masses and classes, and this alone ought to insure his nomination."

"Then you do not believe Governor Morton will win at St. Louis?"

"No, I don't think that Mr. Platt is honestly supporting him. He is using the Governor's name merely to get votes to trade at St. Louis."

"Whom, then, is Mr. Platt really committed to?"

"No one in particular. He will trade his votes where he can get the most credit for them."

Has not every word of that declaration proved true? The only remaining ground of attack upon Mr. Choate is beneath contempt. It appeared in an editorial of the *Sun*, and it was repeated on Monday morning in a letter written for the public press by a member of the legislature, a lawyer acquainted with the facts, a man who ought to have known better. This editorial and this letter taunted Mr. Choate with not taking any active part in the last campaign and criticised him for remaining silent. He was silent. But it was the silence of the darkened home and the saddened life of a bereaved father. All through that summer Choate stood at the bedside of a dying daughter. I shrink from intruding into the privacies of any man's home life, but in the face of this wanton, cruel and cowardly attack, it becomes necessary to lift the veil that hides a strong man's grief from the public gaze. At the height of that campaign, death came to the home of Joseph H. Choate and deprived him of a dearly loved daughter. His friends appreciated the greatness of his grief when they saw him bowed with sorrow and refusing to be comforted because his daughter was not. Such a desolation should have had enough sacredness and pathos in it to have shielded him from this low and brutal calumny. Let us hear no more of that objection.

Yet is there any man who will assert that even then Choate ignored the demands of patriotism and party? Did he not contribute to the full extent of his means to the republican national campaign fund? Did not Mr. Hanna know the cause of Choate's silence and respect and sympathize with it? Did he not know that if it became necessary he could still call and that Choate would respond, however grief-stricken.

Now, men, we are told that this movement is doomed to defeat, because there is in this State a man so powerful, a boss or leader so absolute, that if he decreed he could send to the United States Senate a vagrant from the streets. Mr. Choate is not acceptable to this man. This boss does not approve of Mr. Choate. This leader consults no man. He tolerates no discussion or debate, but in a darkened rear office in the lower part of Broadway, at his own caprice, controlled by no principle, responsible to no one, and following no rule, except perchance it be the famous rule of addition, division and silence, he covertly operates and manipulates the political machine.

I shall read you a text from the New York *Press*, whose republicanism no one will question, and whose editor surely is just as true a protectionist and as mindful of the best interests of the republican party as any of Mr. Choate's critics. Here is what the editor of the *Press* says:

> "The Legislature will do what Mr. Platt directs it to do, because it belongs to him. He can do anything he pleases with it. He can elect himself senator. If he chooses he can name the notorious Lou Payn. Should it so suit his fancy, he could send from New York to the United States Senate an outcast from the party or a vagrant from the streets. And this because the Legislature is his, because he owns it."

We answer that we cannot believe the republican party has sunk as low as the *Press* estimates. If true, it is high time to revolt and free ourselves of such boss rule. We hope that no man owns the republican legislature. We still trust that on the 19th of January, as directed by the federal laws and in pursuance of that State Constitution which was moulded under Choate's direction as President of the Constitutional Convention, the republican majority will obey the will of the people by selecting Choate as our United States Senator.

The candidacy of Mr. Choate is said to be an attempt to rob Mr. Platt of deserved credit and reward, or, as a writer put it, of the crown of statesmanship. Our purpose is not to despoil, but to expose; not to uncrown, but to unmask.

Let us, however, look under the crown and beneath the mask, and see what we find. Can there be any question that the candidacy of Mr. Morton was hopeless from the beginning, and that it was put forward merely as a basis for dickering and negotiations? Was not Choate right in what he said last March? Can any one doubt that if Mr. McKinley and Mr. Hanna had been prepared to make pledges and pay for peace, they could have bought and secured Mr. Platt's enthusiastic support? Do we not all know that McKinley refused to make any bargain for patronage and that he spurned the suggestion? Let me recall a sample of Mr. Platt's statesmanship. I read from an interview with Mr. Platt published in the *Sun* of May 11th, one month before the nomination at St. Louis :

"My opposition to Gov. McKinley proceeds almost entirely from my belief that he will get the republican party into turmoil and trouble. He is not a well-balanced man of affairs. He is not a great man. He is not a trained and educated public man. He is not an astute political leader. He is simply a clever gentleman, much too amiable and much too impressionable to be safely intrusted with great executive office, whose quest for honor happens to have the accidental advantage of the association of his name with the last republican protective tariff."

Yet this man is now put forward as the friend, the admirer, the loyal supporter, if not the discoverer of Mr. McKinley as a presidential candidate.

Again, it is urged that we should elect Mr. Platt as a reward for his heroic services during the last campaign. We know of no services except collecting contributions from corporations and efforts to secure the nomination of such members of the legislature as would be acceptable to him. In all that, he is suspected of having been singularly successful. There only remains the claim as to the gold clause in the St. Louis platform, for which Platt, notwithstanding all his loud pretenses, deserves absolutely no credit. The claim is pure fiction —without any foundation whatever. I shall read what Mr. Hanna said upon this point on June 23d, two days after the convention adjourned:

"The money plank adopted by the convention was in St. Louis long before ex-Senator Platt, Senator Lodge and Mr. Lauterbach arrived. I wish to state most emphatically that the plank defining the party's financial position was advocated by western men, drawn up by western men, and approved in the exact shape in which it was finally adopted, before any man from the East reached St. Louis. The plank, as it was finally approved, went to the convention without any eastern recommendation or suggestion. Finally, I may state with equal emphasis that the plank shown me as representing the eastern sentiment was not adopted by the convention, nor was it anything like the declaration made officially for the republican party, being only two or three sections long."

General Horace Porter, President of the Union League Club, said at the same time:

"On Friday, the 12th of June, five days before the adoption of the platform, I was shown the draft of the solid gold-standard financial plank prepared by Gov. McKinley and his friends. With two insignificant changes of words, and those not affecting the 'gold' clause, that platform was adopted by the convention by a majority of eight to one. No one can rob William McKinley and his immediate advisers of the credit of framing and securing the adoption of our thoroughly admirable financial plank."

And Timothy L. Woodruff, our next Lieutenant Governor, also said:

"I do not believe that Platt had any influence in the making of the gold plank, but the vote for the gold plank would have been just as strong if Mr. Platt had not declared himself in favor of it."

So much for the pretense that Mr. Platt deserves the credit for the gold plank in the St. Louis platform.

It is threatened that those who take part in this movement to elect Mr. Choate will be condemned by Mr. McKinley, and that he intends to hand over all the federal patronage to the man who vilified him seven months ago. What a contemptible estimate of our next President! We know that estimate to be refuted by McKinley's character and his whole career. There he is, waiting to take the presidential oath with the confidence and blessings of the people. He needs no eulogy from us. Shall we send to the Senate the man who abused him? Shall we appoint to represent this State a man who has never risen above the traffic in spoils, a man who will organize in Washington a clearing-house for political tribute, a man who can block, thwart, hold up the new administration at every step, demand terms upon every appointment, exact contributions from every corporation in the United States under the threat and coercion of adverse federal legislation? Would not the presence of such a senator from New York be a blight upon the administration, a dark cloud ever threatening storm and ruin, when God knows we need a clear sky? On the other hand, how auspiciously the new term would begin if you sent Choate to help McKinley? What could you do that would more certainly strengthen the new President and assure success and prosperity for his administration than to send to Washington a man of great talents and unblemished honor, his friend—the foremost citizen of this State?

I shall now ask you to follow me in an examination of two aspects of the political condition within our own party as I believe the situation to exist. According to my lights, this is the vital point and the merit of this whole movement. We have a duty higher than the mere lauding of our choice, as the principles of eternal right and patriotism must ever rise above all other considerations.

The one aspect leads us to inquire whether as Amer icans we can safely submit to the bossism of any man, however pure his motives, however assured of his integrity, however lofty his character? The other aspect requires me to go further and ask you how we come to have such a boss and how he has attained and maintained his political power? Then I shall go still further and higher and impeach that boss as unworthy of being sent to the United States Senate.

In the first place, let us assume that Mr. Platt's methods are entirely legitimate and that his record and talents qualify him to be the leader of the republican party in the Empire State. Is it not element-ary in politics, is it not absolutely certain that the ascendancy of any one man, however pure his motives or high his principles, endangers and threatens the rights of the people? Is it not intolerable that a man elected to no office, with neither evidence nor warrant of trust and confidence on the part of the people, without responsibility to them, shall be permitted to exercise such power and dictate who shall go to the senate? Is not power concentrated in an irresponsible individual always a menace to public liberties? Such a boss, it is perhaps true, may not en-rich himself from the spoils of office and the flood of contributions passing through his fingers; but have we nothing to fear, to apprehend, to dread, from his system, from his practices, from his lust of power? Conceding all that may be said in support of his claim of personal integrity, does not Mr. Platt exercise a power in the administration of the affairs of this State monstrous and tyrannical in the extreme? Does he not exercise a power and exert an influence to which the American people will never submit?

Therefore, if Mr. Platt's character were as high and as unblemished as Mr. Choate's, it would nevertheless be our duty to rebel as republicans in order to save the party itself from the odium and reproach of such methods.

But, there is the other aspect of the case, which is far more serious and odious. We must have courage enough to look the facts in the face, and to ask ourselves some plain questions. Let us come, without flinching, as soon as possible to close fighting and grapple on the real ground of battle. What does Plattism really mean? Whence his power? Why is he said to own the legislature? Why is it felt and believed all over the State that his will is supreme and his control omnipotent? Why is it boasted that he can send himself to the United States Senate or any puppet or figurehead he pleases? How is it possible among a free, spirited and self-respecting people, living under a republican form of government, that one man, who holds no political office, who represents no political principles or doctrines except spoils, who is not responsible to the people, can wield such a power, unlimited, unrestrained, unchecked, accountable to no one?

Since the days of Tweed, a new system of political corruption has come into existence. The individual legislator is now seldom directly bribed. Corporations or individuals seeking protection or valuable charter rights at the hands of a legislature, retain directly or indirectly a recognized political boss and pay him for the service to be rendered. This secures the desired protection or favor. It is pretended that these payments are contributions to the party, but as a matter of fact they are tributes to the fund of the boss, who turns over to the National, State or County Committees as much of the spoil as he sees fit, distributing most of it for the purpose of electing to the legislature his own nominees. In form, it is a contribution to the party; in substance and truth it is bribery or blackmail. Most of these contributions are said to be made by corporations. The items are supposed to be entered on their books under fictitious sundry accounts and hidden from public investigation. In the old days, all contributions to the party were made to the treasurer of the National Committee or the treasurer of the State Committee or the treasurer of the County Committee. There was some accountability. Now they are made to the boss, and there is no accountability, for secrecy is almost always a condition accompanying the so-called contribution. In this way, the New York bosses of both parties are said to collect annually hundreds of thousands of dollars. Mr. Platt is the republican boss, and levies tribute in our party's name. No one ventures to deny the existence of this practice. His champions and defenders concede that this money passes through his hands, but they tell us that we republicans should not object because it is expended solely for the benefit of the republican party. It would, indeed, be interesting to ascertain what proportion of this year's contributions went to the Republican National Committee for legitimate purposes, and what proportion was reserved to assist in electing the present legislature. We are told, however, that we ought not to complain or even to mention this disgraceful fact until we can prove that some part of the money handled by Mr. Platt is devoted to his own enrichment or the enrichment of his henchmen and followers. Does that answer the charge or lessen the guilt? The same plea was advanced on behalf of Mr. Croker. But who knows the truth of the matter? To whom is a statement furnished? To whom is there any responsibility? Who audits the accounts? The professional politicians and bosses of both parties all over the country somehow amass great wealth. Suppose the boss were not so conscientious as we are to understand Mr. Platt is, and, becoming contaminated by handling this fund, were inclined to enrich himself? It was asserted, and perhaps with equal truth, that Mr. Croker used the funds he collected exclusively for the benefit of Tammany Hall.

The principal contributors to this fund are known to be the corporations. Payments are not made by them from any feeling of devotion to the party or its principles. The officers who thus use corporate funds are clearly responsible for their acts. This is a misuse of trust funds; and those who receive are equally guilty—nay, more guilty, for they know that the payments are made in most instances to avoid attack upon corporate property. The time is coming when a fearless investigating committee or district attorney will uncover this whole system, lay it bare, expose it, and put an end forever to the political contributions of corporations to the funds of any boss. "Truth will come to sight"; such practices "cannot be hid" much longer. No corporation has the right to give a dollar for such a purpose, and to do so should be made a criminal offense.

Mr. Platt's great power comes from the handling of this fund, from the levying of tribute directly and indirectly, and we republicans are determined to stop that source of supply and the practice and to destroy that power for the sake of the party itself. We are not willing to wait until an aroused people vents its wrath upon the republican party to punish it for the acts or the crimes of any boss. Our party is as it ever has been the party of the people, the defender of the Constitution and of the rights of property, and any such political methods as we condemn imperil its usefulness and its future.

Tweed in his day was defiant of public opinion. "What are you going to do about it?" he said. But Tilden and O'Conor showed him. Platt likewise is defiant, but the people will find the way to pull him down and destroy his power. When Platt was fighting against McKinley, he issued a statement, published in the *Sun* of May 14, in which he said :

> "I submit to the business men of this country, whose sentiment can always control a nominating convention, that they would better do some thinking between now and the 16th of June on other subjects than this silly twaddle of newspapers about ' bosses ' and ' boss rule.' "

May we not in our turn ask the self-respecting people of this State and their agents at Albany if they had not better do some thinking between now and the 19th of January? Will the people consider this objection to bosses and boss rule as silly twaddle ?

Our liberty is as much endangered by this system of boss rule and corruption as our honor and our national character. It is sapping away the old virile political spirit of Americans and the integrity of our public life. It is undermining the foundations of the republic itself. Unless stopped, the people will lose all confidence in our institutions and sweep them away. The existence of the republican party is endangered by such a corrupt and debasing system of bossism. This night will be memorable if it only shows that the party still has within its own ranks enough courage and spirit to fight for its redemption from boss rule.

Therefore, at the bar of public opinion, I impeach Thomas Collier Platt as unworthy to be sent to the Senate of the United States. I impeach him in the name of the republican party whose trust he has betrayed, whose prestige he has tarnished, whose honor he has sullied. I impeach him as being responsible for a political system conducted in utter defiance of all morality. I impeach him for poisoning political life at the primaries, for debauching the noble science of government, for corrupting and prostituting those who should esteem public office as a public trust. I impeach him in the name of the people of the United States, in the name of both sexes, in the name of every age, in the name of every religion, as the common enemy of all.

ADDRESS OF ELIHU ROOT, Esq.

FELLOW REPUBLICANS:

Mr. Joseph H. Choate is a candidate for election to the Senate of the United States. In the manly and direct fashion which characterizes him, he has placed himself in nomination before the Legislature and the people of the State as a candidate for that high office. I have been asked to come here and say in this public meeting of republican citzens of New York what I think and what I feel regarding his candidacy. I do it cheerfully, because this is the good old-fashioned New York way in which the people express their sentiments and their opinions in order that they may be known by their representatives in the Legislature, in Congress and in the various branches of Government. I do it not under any supposition that we have the election of the Senator in Congress, that you or I can say who shall be the representative of New York in the Senate, but because we are the constituents of some of the members of the Senate and Assembly, because many other constituents and other members of these houses will hear what is said to-night, will read what is said to-night, will find courage to express their views, will be incited, it may be, to range themselves with us in our expression of opinion; and far distant may be the day when the people of the State of New York yield their assent to the proposition that under any circumstances whatever it is an impertinence for any citizen of the State, however humble he may be, however few they may be who agree with him, to express to his representatives in the Legislature of this State his sentiments and his wishes regarding their action. (Applause.)

No legislature, no governor, no congress and no president is the superior of the people of the United States. (Applause.) They go to their high places to register and execute the will of their constituents, and the way in which that will is made known is by the free, voluntary and spontaneous expression of individual opinion, however humble each individual may be. (Applause.)

For such an expression of opinion we are met to-night. I have come here to wage no war, to attack no one, but to say what is in my mind as furnishing a reason why, in my judgment, the members of the legislature of the State of New York would do wisely to vote for Mr. Choate as Senator in Congress to represent the State. (Applause.)

He is a candidate, and I suppose we are all for him. Certainly we would not have come through the storm of this inclement night if we had not been for him. I am sure that I am for him for reasons.

The first reason is to be found in the necessary answer to the question: What member of the legislature can be found who, if he had great interests at stake himself, if his life, his liberty, his property, the deepest and dearest interests of those for whom he cares were at stake, would accept the service of any other man in this State if he could get the advocacy and support of Joseph H. Choate? (Applause.)

I do not say that he is the only man in this State of New York fit to be Senator in Congress. There are many others who would well and worthily fill that position. There is no other avowed candidate for the place. (Applause.) There doubtless will be, but no man can tell who they will be. It is probable that there will be candidates emerging in the future who are not fit for the position; it is highly probable that there will be others who are fit for the position, but I do undertake to say from what we have seen of this gentleman as he has gone in and out among us for more than a generation, as we have watched the splendid achievements of his brilliant talents, as we have known the sterling qualities of his estimable character that there cannot be found in the length and breadth of this State or of any other state between the Atlantic and the Pacific a man more worthy to be Senator in Congress than Mr. Choate. (Applause.)

I am for him not only because he is my dear friend of many years, but because I have a pride in the Republican party and I wish it to be well and gloriously represented; because I have a pride in my state in which I was

born and have lived all my life, and I wish it to be well
and gloriously represented ; because I have the interest of
my country at heart, and I wish it to have the services of
its best and noblest citizens in these coming years which
I feel are to be years of trial.

I believe he is the best man for the place. He is wise.
Can proof be required of it better than the stream of the
wise, the most successful, the most sagacious, the most
acute of the citizens of this great city who seek the doors
of his office day by day to ask his advice upon the most
intricate, difficult and important questions. He is able.
Can better proof be required than the stream of applicants
for his service, who come from every city and from every
State, wherever the greatest and most important questions
are to be determined by our highest courts. His mind is
stored with learning, the wisdom of past generations, of
great minds who have thought upon questions of government, of politics, of economy. His mind is trained by
literature, by familiarity with the great writers, the great
orators, the great philosophers of past ages, and this
has given to him that wonderful style with which we are
so familiar as clear, as direct, as simple, as effective, as
ever proceeded from the mouth of any man within the
hearing of any one within this hall. (Applause.)

He is not only wise and learned from books : he knows
the book of life. He knows human character, and, with
a rare insight, plays upon it in the interests of the causes
which he represents as skillfully as the born genius in
music touches the strings of his instrument. Before a
court, before a jury, before any assemblage whatever, this
wise and sagacious man, with his keen insight into the
human heart and character, touches in all ways the true
chords that he wishes to respond.

He has eloquence. He has the keen, incisive wit
that clears the way in the dullest understanding, for the
bitterly cold and certain logic that proceeds always direct
from certain premises to irrefutable conclusion. He has
the wonderful power to adorn the cold hard processes of
reasoning with the gentle and graceful play of humor.

All the qualities which go to make up the statesman, the legislator. the orator, the mover and the wielder of men, whether it be in the forum or upon the rostrum: whether it be before courts, before public assemblages, or in the halls of legislation, this townsman of ours combines in his own person. And he has a high and serene courage which fails under no circumstances, and in no emergency. He does not carry his heart upon his sleeve for daws to peck at, but those who know him know that no man ever surpassed him in the quality of faithful friendship. When his time comes—far distant may it be—to render his account, he can say, like the young Cameronian hero of romance: "God, so do to me, and more also if ever I gave my back to a foe or my shoulder to a friend all the days of my life." (Applause.)

I repeat the question, what member of the Legislature of this State would accept inferior service if in an hour of great emergency his dearest interests were involved, and he could secure the aid of this great advocate?

There are some things in which one dispenses business and opportunity as a matter of favor. There are some bits of business which are given to nephews and the sons of friends and personal and social acquaintances, because one man can do them as well as another, and it is a very good thing to help along a friend pecuniarily or in his profession; but when a man's life is at stake. when his liberty is at stake, when his property is at stake, how quickly all that vanishes. How quickly he seeks the man who can save him, and accepts no inferior service.

Now, what is the cause that the State of New York has? What service does the State of New York require from its Senator in Congress? Is it a holiday procession, this Senate of the United States, in these years now to come, to which one shall send some favored associate to be displayed in the trappings and to bear the honors of office? Is this a piece of business which is to be given as a favor to some one who will profit by it? Is it something which is to be used to please a friend? Or is it something serious and earnest? Why, how can one ask the question? The flags

are hardly yet withdrawn from our streets under which
marched the procession of the people of New York of all
parties, of all creeds, of all shades of previous opinion,
united with one great effort, to face and meet manfully a
common danger. The sounds of the voice of patriotism
have hardly died away since the great conflict of No-
vember was brought to a conclusion. Thousands of
our fellow citizens, belonging to the party which we
insist is inferior to ours in patriotism, in willingness
to sacrifice itself in the love of country, turned their
backs upon their party in that contest, sacrificed
such hopes of political preferment as they may have
had, and made common cause with their political
adversaries for the common good of our beloved country. (Applause.) We have heard a hundred times
within the last few months the indisputable truth
that the crisis which we have just faced was the most
serious crisis which America has ever had to meet since
the constitution of the United States was first established—
more serious than the terrible stress of civil war in 1861.
We believed it, did we not? It is true, is it not, that the
people of America were obliged to face the assaults of an
enemy more deadly than foreign or than civil war could
produce? Assaults upon national honor; assaults upon
the sacred right of contract; assaults upon the independence of our judiciary; assaults upon the power of the
Union to enforce its own laws; assaults upon the very
basis of our social condition; assaults by men who sought
to tear down the government of the United States in order
to set up another and a different government in its place!
Patriotism has but lately ruled in all the hearts of good
and honest Americans. A great victory has been won.
But, is the war over? Ah! no. We know it is not. The
prosperity for which we looked so hopefully has not yet
come, and it has not come because but one battle has been
gained, and the war is still on and still to be fought out; because the hosts that were assaulting the citadel of national
life and honor are gathering again for the assault, and the

first battle-field where they are to be met is the Senate of the United States. (Applause.)

From that high vantage ground this year and next year, and every year until the election of 1900, will go forth loud-sounding notes of heresy and error to the misguided millions who voted for Bryan on last election day. In that body of power and influence the financial legislation which our country so sorely needs to be wise and prudent is prevented by Senators of the United States; in that body to-day trembles perhaps the dreadful balance between war and peace, with all the untold horrors that a wrong decision may bring. Is it an opportunity to oblige a friend, to decorate a friend? Ah, no,—the duty of patriotism, the duty of self-interest, the duty of plain common sense, require that to that battlefield. to that point of stress and conflict, this great State, with one-tenth of the population of the Union, with far more than one-tenth of its wealth, with its enormous commercial and manufacturing and agricultural interests, with more at stake than any other part of the Union,—this great State should send the best, the ablest, the greatest of its warriors to fight the battle of the Constitution, of the law, of national honor, of the independence of the judiciary, of our social system, of independent Americanism. (Applause.) Now is the opportunity for the people of New York to show that they care for our country, and are willing to render it aid in hours of trial ; now is the opportunity for the people of New York to show that they are really fit to govern themselves (Applause) by doing, through the best and the strongest that they can send, good work for the cause of the Union and of national honor. (Applause.) Ah, how would the wise and good men of the senate welcome a coadjutor like Choate? How gladly would Aldrich and Allison, and Sherman, and Hoar, and Frye, and Hale, and all the other of the stalwart and staunch Republicans who have been fighting the battles of honesty and honor against the crowd of repudiators and agitators and anarchists, welcome the assistance of Choate! (Applause.) How soon may the time come when before the great questions which that body has to determine in the near future, questions affecting the very life of our Union, the honor of our country, the perpetuity of our institutions, the continuance of our social status,—how soon may the time come when every father, every good law-abiding citizen of this State will be ready to cry, " Oh, for one hour of that clarion voice to speak from that high vantage ground the great truths on which our Union, our honor and our country rest! Oh, for one thrust of that keen and incisive wit to puncture the false pretense of error. (Great applause.) Oh, for one American like Choate in the Senate of the United States to do unto the heresies of dishonor, of national degradation, what Webster did for nullification, what Sumner did for human slavery."

Our voice in this great contest is but the voice of one crying in the wilderness. Members of the Legislature are elected, they are about to take their places, they are about to declare their choice. But one thing we can do. We can say so loudly, so often, what we think it is the duty of the State of New York to do, that if our fellow-citizens agree with us they, too, will take up the cry; they, too, will send the message to their representatives at Albany, and that body, which is always really responsive to public opinion, if made to believe in its existence and to realize what it is—that that body will rise to the true dignity of the opportunity, will realize the duty which is before it, and will do for the State of New York what the plain interests of our common country and the interests of their constituents demand—send to the Senate the best man for the performance of the great, important duties which are to be performed.

GENERAL WAGER SWAYNE'S REMARKS.

GENTLEMEN:

The little that I have to say to you is concerned with a very direct and specific proposition: it is that the primaries of the Republican party in the City of New York are just as dishonest as the supremacy of the Republican machine may require that they shall be (applause), and that this dishonesty, rising through the body politic, concentres in corruption at its head (applause); and that this meeting is called in aid of an attempt to end that state of things with which it is not possible that there shall be any compromise (applause); and this, as I have said, is a specific proposition, and it is not put forward as a general statement to which the credulous assent of any man is asked.

A few months ago a pamphlet was put forward and freely offered to the perusal of the citizens of New York. I have a copy in my hand; other copies are easily within your reach. Precisely the statement that I have made in your hearing is made in this pamphlet, and it is supported by facts and figures, names and dates; and it is signed by twenty-five Republicans of New York City, and among them Joseph H. Choate. (Applause.)

Now, those gentlemen have made in this pamphlet a specific statement to the general effect that the Republican primaries in the City of New York are dishonest, and they give the numbers of men found in each district, the numbers of names fraudulently upon the roll in each district; they challenge investigation; they submit all manner of reports; and they make this statement deliberately over their signatures, placing upon themselves the alternative either of dishonest or reckless accusation or else of being exponents of a carefully ascertained truth. They show apparently beyond dispute, that members of the Republican County Committee in sufficient numbers to fix the character and control the conduct of that Committee have obtained their membership by fraud.

Now, it is not necessary to a movement that is based

upon that state of facts, designed for its eradication, that the moral character or the political behavior of any man be made the subject of vituperative statements. Be the man never so honest, if the responsibility for that state of facts rests on that man, his continuance in political authority is a damage, and a just one, to his party, and a danger to his country and to every good interest that his country has in charge. (Applause.)

Hence, we have, if you please, in this a specific starting point. These statements, so made, as the result of most careful and laborious and honest investigation, were laid before the Governor of this State, the Honorable Levi P. Morton. He sent them back for investigation and report to the Republican County Committee. If that County Committee had been composed of men in no degree implicated with these frauds, of high-minded and disinterested men, or if, being such as they are, they had replied with other facts and figures reasonably supporting a different judgment, certainly I would not be here at this time. Instead of that, this County Committee is shown by this book to have been largely composed of men who held place in the committee as the result of dishonesty at those very primary elections.

Even then, if they had come back with a refutation, even an attempted specific refutation of these accusations of fraud, the matter would have stood upon a different basis from that upon which it stands at this time. Instead of that they pooh-poohed these statements, and from that day until now they have never spoken of them except in terms of general denial or general indifference or contempt.

Now, if a notoriously dishonest person charges a man of good reputation with dishonesty, and doesn't make his case good with specific facts, the man who is charged may treat the accusation with contemptuous silence. But is there a man in the City of New York who can afford to have a damaging statement made about him, with the facts specifically presented and signed by twenty-five men such as these and treat it with contemptuous silence? Is there a man in the City of New York who, if such a statement were made about him specifically, by such men, or for that matter, by one of them, and he failed to reply, you would not feel that he had deservedly lost your confidence and respect? That is a plain statement of the facts upon which this situation stands; the details are open to you.

What followed in this case? There was an appeal to the County Committee, as I have said. When the County Committee refused to take any notice of those charges and continued in its membership the men whose individual participation in those frauds and individual fruits of those frauds is here disclosed, then for a right-minded Republican there came an irrepressible conflict between the Republican party and that County Committee, and the State Machine, which, as you will presently see, has adopted all its frauds, and it continues to this day.

Well, what next? An appeal to the State Committee, and the same species of treatment. What no man in this city of any character whatever could afford to disregard if put forth with like circumstance by one man of decent reputation, first a County Committee and then a State Committee treats as wholly unworthy of consideration or reply, although more than five thousand resident Republicans had, in appealing to the State Committee, joined in the request already made by the committee of twenty-five that some action looking to the establishment of decency should be taken.

What next? This careful, thorough and unquestioned exposure was denounced by the machine as an ignominious failure; it had accomplished nothing. Let us see for a moment whether it did or not? A presidential election was impending; it was the next thing to be looked after, the first result of it to be secured, if possible, by whoever cared for honesty in the Republican party was that for the next four years if the Republican candidates should be elected the Republican machine that had espoused and adopted these frauds should not be able to strengthen itself by unlimited drafts on federal patronage, saying to the newly elected President of the United States: "Do now as we ask, because we put you here." Therefore, there was a careful and intelligent study of the presidential field to find who it might be who could be best supported as a presidential candidate, with confidence that if he were elected he would not be controlled by the Republican machine in the State of New York as to matters in this City. And as careful a study as a lawyer gives to the evidence in an important case brought conviction to the minds of many men in New York that the best man for that purpose, the man who if he were elected President would stand most firmly against the corrupt influences of the machine, was William McKinley of Ohio (applause), and in that way the facts herein disclosed led to the calling of a meeting at Cooper Institute in this city to start a movement which should plainly signify to the Republican Convention at St. Louis, and to its candidate when elected that the machine was not in exclusive control of the Republican vote in the State of New York, and that if its candidates were elected by the vote of New York he would not owe that vote exclusively to the machine. It was not at that time a pleasant or a popular thing to do, but it seemed like a duty to honesty in Republican administration in this city and in this state, and it was done, and the result has proved it was effective. How well the shot told could be seen by the answering volley of abuse of Major McKinley with which the Machine immediately replied in the newspapers it controls.

What next? There were subsequent primaries and they were naturally just as dishonest as those commented upon here and more so. Some man said: " We can do nothing; let us drop it." What does that mean? Suppose there were dishonesty in the State of Oregon in Republican councils and management and administration there, what would that mean to a Republican in New York? Would it not mean that in laboring for his country through the medium of his party he makes himself the companion of knaves? Would it not mean that the Republicans of Oregon are compelling the Republicans in New York to be co-laborers in a tainted party?

Would it not mean neglecting the fire of fraud that needs only to be left to burn unchecked and it will speedily consume the entire body politic? The truth is: that a man cannot be a Republican and know these things, and not continue to do his level best against them. It was said, "Get up a rival organization; go to the primaries, and beat these people at their own game." There is a difficulty about that, and it is this: that any body of men organized for the pursuit of a given object and getting their living out of that pursuit can clean out any time another corresponding body of men pursuing the same object, but obliged to earn their living in the meantime. (Laughter and applause.) You cannot do that. The way to stop fraud at the primaries is to have a reserve force of public sentiment that is strong enough, when the fraud is pointed out, to expel from the convention the man who is there by fraud. When fraud becomes profitless men do not practice fraud. (Applause.)

It is easy to see that this particular variety of fraud corrupts all the body politic, for primaries make delegates, delegates make conventions, conventions make candidates, candidates are the limitations of elections and elections are the seat of power. That is the whole story and it is very simple. Therefore, it comes back again to the point that we have dishonest primaries in the city of New York, and, so long as we have them, the Republican party in the city is of no value, but is, on the contrary, an injury to Republicans throughout the country. (Applause.) There is nothing, there never was anything on the face of the earth, and I think there never will be anything, quite so wonderful as a great nation exercising its functions for the protection of the weak, the relief of the afflicted, the diffusion of learning, the assistance of the poor, the promotion of industry and the maintenance of justice; and yet all those things are struck at under our system of government when there is dishonesty at the root of a political party that sometimes controls and always largely influences the operations of the nation. That is what it means, gentlemen. In fighting it, against any odds whatever, there is nothing of the crank; it is intensely practical. Although the State Committee contemptuously dismissed the protest out of which this movement grew, it is well known that the State Machine did not dare to nominate for Governor the man it would have set up had there been no opposition in the field within the party. It is as yet by no means clear that they have not builded better than they knew for uprightness of administration in this State. That by itself, if it prove to be true, will richly repay whatever the protest cost.

I have already suggested to you that this evidence of dishonest primaries was enough to set on foot and support a movement which tended to reduce the influence and in a degree paralyze the action of the New York Republican machine at the Convention in St. Louis, and tended to bring about the nomination of the man who, in the best judgment of those that organized that movement, was the best adapted of all the candidates and the most to be relied upon to resist the influence of the machine in this city and in this State. Within the past week a reputable gentleman in this city told me that before Major McKinley's nomination he happened to call upon him at his home in Canton and found him with a copy of this pamphlet in his hand.

Now, gentlemen, what next? When the machine found—and the machine is nothing but the aggregate result of dishonest primaries (if the primaries were honest the machine would be impossible)—when the machine found that the man whom it had derided in the newspapers, as has to-night been read in your hearing, was the chosen of the people for their President, what next? What next about the federal patronage? The Senate of the United States has a great countervailing and counterbalancing influence upon the President of the United States. It was so designed and is so fixed in the Constitution of the United States. If any President of the United States is a man with whom terms can be made and bargains driven, a man in the Senate of the United States is in position to make those terms and drive those bargains. Therefore it is that every one of you who has in the least degree an intelligent knowledge of public affairs in the State of New York at this time knows that there are two elements in the Republican party contending just now as to who shall be sent to the Senate this winter to represent New York. It may very well be that as great, wise, good and true a man as Mr. Choate cannot be sent to the Senate of the United States by the present legislature of New York. But the matter does not end there. This movement will in any case make a difference in the Senate of the United States. It is going to make a difference in the power and potency of the Republican machine in the City of New York and in the State of New York whether or not the man who is sent to the Senate of the United States shall go there with the whole of the State of New York behind him—so far, at least, as the Republican party is concerned—or shall go there stamped with the brand of the machine upon his brow, and carrying such weight only as may belong to one who is known to have been sent there by the machine and for its purposes alone. (Applause.)

That is what Mr. Choate meant when in response to the urgent solicitations of his friends he said he would stand as a candidate if he did not get one legislative vote. (Applause.) To whatever extent you support him, to whatever extent the people of this city support him, to whatever extent the members of the legislature may support him, to precisely that extent whoever is elected as an anti-Choate man will go to the Senate of the United States, as has been said this evening, not discovered but exposed. It seems to me that is rational. We had among those who signed the paper calling attention to those frauds a great man, a wise man, a good man, a true man, a pure man. We said to him, "Let us try at least to send you to the Senate, and if we bring upon you only ridicule, still bear it, because the ridicule will come from evil sources and what you do will be serviceable to the right." We have not mistaken our man. It was his phrase, not ours, when he said he would stand as a candidate if he did not get a vote.

Gentlemen, whoever wants to accomplish a moral result in this world must be prepared for failure in the immediate result; but it does not always follow from the fact that the preparation has been made that the fruition of failure will be achieved. What we entertained as a forlorn hope at the beginning is no longer forlorn. Look at the names of the men, look at the organizations that are coming day by day to the front in the City of New York, look at the list of names in this afternoon's paper, all supporters of Joseph H. Choate. In Brooklyn—Dr. Storrs, Mayor Schieren, Benjamin D. Silliman, and a whole list of names like that? Don't they insure this result in the minds of the people of the State of New York, that a man who goes to the Senate of the United States against the protest of those men will go there, known widely as they are known, as the exponent of all those things in politics against which those men have protested! You and I, gentlemen, lodge also our protests, the result is with the people. Sometimes the people are slow, but they are not permanently wrong. I thank you for your attention.

LETTERS READ AT THE MEETING.

LETTER OF REV. RICHARD S. STORRS OF BROOKLYN.

DECEMBER 22D, 1896.

MY DEAR SIR :—

I regret extremely that it is not in my power to accept the invitation to the meeting proposed to be held in New York to-morrow evening, for furthering the election of Mr. Choate to the United States Senate. Imperative engagements at home detain me; and I can only hope that if a similar meeting shall be held in Brooklyn in the coming days I may be able to take part in it.

The matter is not one which concerns Mr. Choate alone or chiefly, or his personal friends, but the State and the Nation. The office of Senator at Washington,—representing a great State in the council of the States,—is surely one which demands the highest qualities of mind and spirit. An unblemished reputation is of course the first essential condition of fitness for it, with entire freedom from suspicion of any crafty and mercenary manipulation of local politics for personal ends. But beyond these are needed the highest order of intellectual ability, a matured and commanding civil wisdom, the power of influencing others by convincing and eloquent speech, a fearless and an uplifting temper which abides on high levels, the noble patriotism which consults the welfare of the whole country, with a sense of relationship to the great history in which the Senate has borne aforetime so distinguished a part.

It is not often that a man can be found qualified for so exalted an office, and at the same time willing to accept, at whatever private sacrifice, its manifold labors and vast responsibilities. The opportunity presented when such a man appears is one which tests democratic institutions. To fail to improve it, and, instead of improving it, to place the honor and power of the State in hands inadequate or unfit for the majestic trust, would be at any time more than a calamity, more than a blunder, it would involve disgrace for all concerned in the evil work.

Especially must this be the consequence at a time so critical as the present, when gravest questions are before the nation for illuminating discussion and final decision; questions affecting our permanent public and private interests, as well as our important and far-reaching foreign relations. At a time like this, to have the State of New York consent to be represented in the Senate by a dexterous and ambitious manager of the caucus, when the opportunity is at hand for placing a really great man, honest and incorruptible, in the seat of Seward or Silas Wright, it would almost make one despair of the Republic. Certainly the honor and the moral coherence of the Republican party would suffer heavily through any such action.

With all my heart, therefore, I am with you in the effort to have the State rise to the level of the great occasion, and send Mr. Choate to counsel and speak for it in the Senate.

Faithfully yours,

RICHARD S. STORRS.

Mr. EDMUND WETMORE,
President, etc.

LETTER OF HON. SETH LOW, President of Columbia University.

DECEMBER 23D, 1896.

PAUL D. CRAVATH, Esq.,
Chairman.

MY DEAR SIR:—

Three years ago, the Republican Party in this State made Mr. Choate a member of the Constitutional Convention and elected him President of the Convention. In this capacity Mr. Choate splendidly vindicated, by his fidelity to the duties of the position, by his dignity, by his tact, by his good judgment, and by his great ability in debate, the sagacity of the Party in selecting him for this high and influential position. There is little doubt that the people of the State confirmed the choice of the Party in this case with satisfaction and enthusiasm. The State having thus received good service from Mr. Choate in this conspicuous position, I believe that it would be good judgment to avail of his great abilities again by electing him to the Senate of the United States. Some men have the gift of measuring up to their opportunities, whatever they may be. Such an one I think Mr. Choate will show himself to be in the Senate Chamber of the United States, should he be elected to that high office. Therefore, I cordially endorse and support his candidacy and join with pleasure in the movement to urge him upon the Legislature for the Senatorship about to become vacant.

Respectfully,

SETH LOW.

LETTER OF WILLIAM ALLEN BUTLER, Esq.

54 WALL STREET, NEW YORK,
Dec. 23d, 1896.

EDMUND WETMORE, Esq.,
        President of the Choate Club.

MY DEAR SIR:

I regret that I am disabled by a cold from taking part in the meeting to be held this evening in aid of Mr. Choate's Candidacy for the United States Senate, which I think ought to commend itself to our incoming Legislature for the following, among other reasons:

1st. The Senate of the United States, despite the just criticism and censure it has provoked, is still a most essential and important factor in our system of free constitutional government. Aside from the Legislative powers which it shares with the House of Representatives, the more important Executive offices can be filled only with its advice and consent, and it exercises, in conjunction with the President, the Treaty-making power. The fore-most names in American Statesmanship are connected with its annals. Out of the twenty-three Presidents of the United States, thirteen have presided over, or been members of the Senate. Of these the first was John Adams and the last Benjamin Harrison. Our own State has in former days sent its most distinguished public men to the Senate. Silas Wright when he resigned in 1844 to become Governor of New York was its most esteemed member. Since then, William H. Seward, John A. Dix, Edwin D. Morgan, and Roscoe Conkling, not to mention others, have been fit representatives of the Empire State in the Senate. The highest personal character, a large experience in public affairs, a knowledge of Constitutional and Parliamentary law, skill in debate and wisdom in council, are among the indispensable requisites for a fit discharge of the duties of a Senator.

2nd. It is conceded that Mr. Choate possesses all the requisite qualifications. If he is willing to serve the State as a Senator in Congress, his eminent fitness ought to make his election sure. There is special need now of well-trained jurists in the Senate. The active, intelligent and able lawyers who will so largely control our next State Legislature know perfectly well that Mr. Choate is the best and worthiest man New York can at the present juncture send to the Senate. They know, too, that for a lawyer the indispensable requisite for his standing and re-pute is the esteem and respect of the members of his own profession. Any lawyer who casts his vote in the coming Senatorial election at the dictation of partisan leadership or for selfish political ends, instead of the highest public interest, deserves to forfeit the good opinion of the Bar of New York.

3rd. The present situation of the country demands new safeguards against national perils. Sound men are just as necessary as sound money. We have escaped a great disaster by the united efforts of citizens who, in the face of threatened dangers, made party subservient to patriotism. Certainly we should not fall back upon the machinery of party as the rule of action when the popular will has declared, as in this State, in an unexampled way, that the safety of the Republic is the highest law for political leaders and managers as well as for the people at large.

4th. There is no worthy candidacy in opposition to that of Mr. Choate. The public seems to have adjusted itself to the idea that the action of the Legislature in the election of a United States Senator is to be that of a voting machine, set in motion by a single hand to register the decree of a single will. If the Legislature of New York has come at last to such base uses, the fact should be made clear and patent and not disguised under subterfuges and evasions. If a candidacy which in 1881 was a source of political disturbance and disquiet until it shrank out of sight into a self-chosen obscurity, is to be rehabilitated in 1897 as a necessary outcome of a restored party supremacy, it is not unreasonable to challenge and scrutinize its claims. Candor and common sense, as well as the settled law which governs political issues, demand this. Public men must, as to public matters, be judged by this record, and when the issue is as to a claim for the highest recognition and reward, the burden of proof is on the claimant to show superior fitness and good ground for the preferment which he seeks. The Legislature of 1897 is to be the arbiter of this issue, and all right-minded men, as it seems to me, would regard with alarm and indignation, however repressed or hindered in their utterance by party ties or affiliations, a result which would inevitably lower the standard of the public service in its most exalted sphere. This peril can only be averted by the election of Mr. Choate.

Yours very truly,

WM. ALLEN BUTLER.

LETTER OF HON. SHERMAN S. ROGERS OF BUFFALO.

BUFFALO, 22nd Decr., 1896.

W. D. GUTHRIE, Esq.,
   & PAUL D. CRAVATH, Esq.,
     for Committee.

GENTLEMEN :

I greatly regret my inability to attend the Carnegie Hall meeting tomorrow evening for I most warmly favor Mr. Choate's candidacy and would gladly say so on that occasion with whatever emphasis I could command.

Two things seem so clear at this time that I cannot imagine how any good citizen, and especially any good *Republican* citizen, can fail to see them. The first is, that the State of New York stands in urgent need of a great Senator. The other is, that in Mr. Choate the need would be fully supplied. Why, then, should he not be nominated?

Most sincerely Yours,

SHERMAN S. ROGERS.

LETTER OF REV. R. S. MACARTHUR, D.D.

CALVARY BAPTIST CHURCH.
57th St., bet. 6th & 7th Aves.
PASTOR'S RESIDENCE,
358 West 57th St.

NEW YORK, Dec. 21, 1896.

MR. PAUL D. CRAVATH,
   DEAR SIR:

Yours of the 19th inst. I answered last Saturday evening verbally, as I was so engaged at the moment I could not write. I appreciate the honor of the invitation given me to address the meeting to be held at Carnegie Music Hall in favor of the election of Mr. Choate to the United States Senate, but an engagement to lecture that evening in another part of the City forbids my acceptance of the invitation.

I hail with joy the possibility of Mr. Choate's election to the Senate. His election would confer honor upon the City, the State and the Country. The presence in the Senate of a man of his wide learning, great eloquence and high character would remind the country of the Senate's great days when its walls echoed with the patriotic eloquence of Sumner, Webster and men of like character.

The election of Mr. Choate would give us the opportunity of putting a scholar, a patriot and a statesman into the Senate of the United States. The Senate much needs men of his character and worth. Every instinct of patriotism should lead all true Americans now to favor the election of a genuine statesman. The mere politician ought not to be in demand when a senator from the great State of New York is to be elected. Our State is much in need of senatorial representation worthy of the population, wealth and character of the Empire State.

Very truly yours,
R. S. MacArthur.

LETTER OF HON. MATTHEW HALE OF ALBANY.

Law Offices of Hale, Bulkeley & Tennant,
25 North Pearl Street,
Albany, N. Y.

December 21, 1896.

Paul D. Cravath, Esq.,
107 East 37th Street, New York.

Dear Sir:

I regret that I could not accept your invitation to attend the Choate mass meeting Wednesday night. As a citizen of the State of New York, interested in her prosperity and greatness and wishing that she might be worthily represented in the Senate of the United States, it would have afforded me much satisfaction to aid in the expression of a public sentiment in favor of the election as Senator of a man of the high attainments, the great ability and the conceded integrity of Mr. Choate. No one who knows him can question his rare qualifications for the position. The mention of his name takes us back to the traditions of the times when such men as Webster, Rufus Choate, Clay, Calhoun, Silas Wright, Marcy, Dix and Seward were members of that body. * * *

Wishing you the greatest success in your meeting Wednesday evening and in the hope that the Legislature may see that the honor and credit of the State can be best promoted by the election of Mr. Choate to the Senate, I remain

Very truly yours,

MATTHEW HALE.

RESOLUTIONS UNANIMOUSLY ADOPTED BY THE MEETING

Resolved, That the Republican voters of the City of New York at this meeting assembled, recognize the paramount importance of electing as United States Senator from the State of New York, the Hon. Joseph H. Choate, who as leader of the American Bar, and our foremost constitutional lawyer, is peculiarly qualified to represent the State of New York during the critical period through which the Nation is now passing;

Resolved further, That we pledge our earnest efforts to the support of Mr. Choate's candidacy, and request our representatives in the Legislature to vote for him;

Resolved further, That a copy of these resolutions be sent to each member of the Legislature.

www.ingramcontent.com/pod-product-compliance
Lightning Source LLC
Chambersburg PA
CBHW032134080426
42733CB00008B/1065